PAST PRESENT AND THE FUTURE

BOOK OF THREE POEMS

AYUSH SAHU

Copyright © Ayush Sahu
All Rights Reserved.

This book has been published with all efforts taken to make the material error-free after the consent of the author. However, the author and the publisher do not assume and hereby disclaim any liability to any party for any loss, damage, or disruption caused by errors or omissions, whether such errors or omissions result from negligence, accident, or any other cause.

While every effort has been made to avoid any mistake or omission, this publication is being sold on the condition and understanding that neither the author nor the publishers or printers would be liable in any manner to any person by reason of any mistake or omission in this publication or for any action taken or omitted to be taken or advice rendered or accepted on the basis of this work. For any defect in printing or binding the publishers will be liable only to replace the defective copy by another copy of this work then available.

Contents

Foreword

The first poem 'the past' tells about a man who failed in his exams because of lack of interest and also because of the accompany of bad mates in his lifes.He now wish to go to his past and to change his fortune. The second poem 'what I have' is set on the theme of child labour. In this modern generation also we have some evil things one of them which is chhild labour. The poet wanders in a town where at one place he sees children paying while at the other shop the children were working wearing dirty dresses. The third and the last poem tells about the a man who travels in speed and unfortunately met with an accident. He thoughts to enjoy his life and not to increase bank balance which is now of no use for him.Hope that you like the poems.

1. THE PAST

Standing at a point, to be call turning,

In front of the hall where the consequence use to.

Tears scrolling down, with the heart burning

Future ambitions turned blank and the answer no.

My past holds no value, as I haven't much bid,

The people I chose, weren't good to with.

Things seem to be bad, wasn't actually were,

I was the cause behind my choice utter.

Wish once again, go to my past there,

Reading the course, and the quotes fair.

Lies in front the black future vast,

Once again want me in my past.

• 4 •

2. WHAT I HAVE

I trudged through a town,

While the sky was some orange and brown.

I wasn't happy, as I was distraught,

Behind my that happiness, there was a cause.

Down I came to a shop,

Children there running with gallop.

And laughing under the roof,

I smiled, as I saw them aloof.

As I moved a little,

I came to a cotton mill.

Children there with messy fabric,

Without fun or school as I compared to them.

Every situation doesn't holds one face,

One with land barren, and the other with pave.

After contemplating, I tried to find my gloom's base,

I never thought about, what do I have

3. NEED, OF THE SPEED

After a long sleep, when I opened my eyes,

Found almost everyone, surrounded by me.

Don't know why it was for me, difficult to rise,

As someone special was missing that night.

Behind me, a car turned into trash,

Inside me, as the cause of the crash.

I came to remember my past,

The horrified sleep that I got.

Flying like an eagle,

In front came a truck.

Now lying as a beagle,

My breathe got stuck.

Nothing now left, including myself,

I have only what I have spent.

But I was engaged in balance, as someone counselled,

What was the need of the speed, now I felt

www.ingramcontent.com/pod-product-compliance
Lightning Source LLC
Chambersburg PA
CBHW020858160726
47993CB00004B/1717